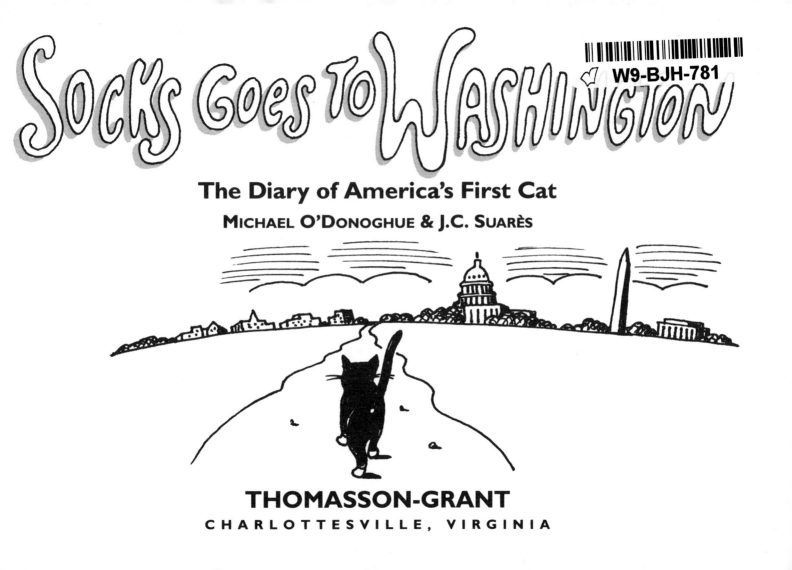

SOCKS GOES TO WASHINGTON

The Diary of America's First Cat

MICHAEL O'DONOGHUE & J.C. SUARÈS

THOMASSON-GRANT
CHARLOTTESVILLE, VIRGINIA

To Cheryl and Nina
"The sweetest kittens have the sharpest claws."

Published by Thomasson-Grant, Inc.

Library of Congress
Cataloging-in-Publication Data available.
ISBN 1-56566-042-0

00 99 98 97 96 95 94 93 5 4 3 2

Any inquiries should be directed to:
Thomasson-Grant, Inc.
One Morton Drive, Suite 500,
Charlottesville, Virginia 22903-6806
(804) 977-1780

THOMASSON-GRANT

My name is SOCKS.

Socks may be a silly name,
but it's better than TIPPER.

I live in the White House.

my room

I'm America's First Cat.

I have a busy schedule.

My cat dish once belonged
to Calvin Coolidge.

I love it here. This is a very old house with more mice than most people realize.

there are some great spiders in the Lincoln Bedroom.

It's fun to sharpen your claws on priceless and irreplaceable furniture.

I have a bulletproof carrying case.

When I'm bored, I break
Nancy Reagan's china.

I hate the helicopter.

the inauguration was fun. There were lots of balloons for me to pop, and I looked up Stevie Nicks' dress.

I'm glad Teddy Roosevelt isn't around any more.

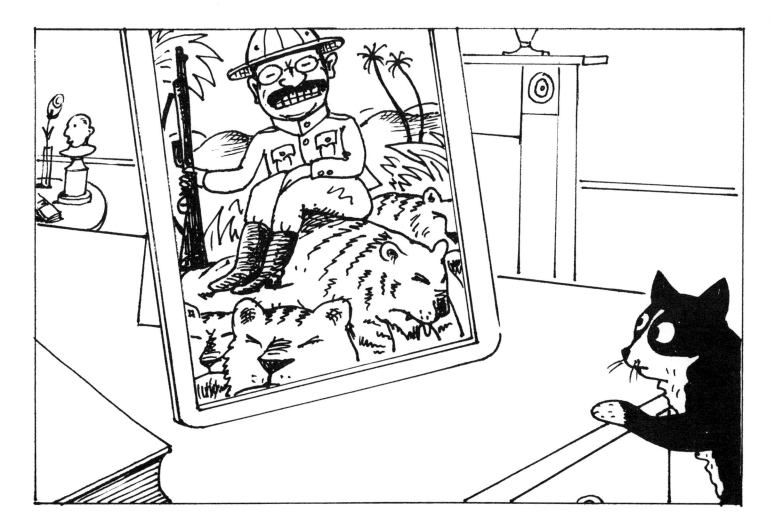

I like to scare the Secret Service guys by racing up and down the hall for no apparent reason.

An old horseshoe pit makes
a fabulous litter box.

Sometimes I dabble in foreign policy.

HAIL TO THE CHIEF hurts my ears.

I'm looking forward to clawing the drapes in the Green Room.

the President threw me out of his office this morning, so I took a whiz in his jogging shoe.

The President is mad at me because I got tuna fish on his power tie.

Nothing peps up a cabinet meeting more than a dead mole.

the Marines hate it when
I drool on their shoes.

Every Wednesday, Chelsea and
I watch 90210.

Just once I wish Hillary would stay home and bake me some cookies.

Sometimes I chase my tail. It's a lot like trying to balance the budget.

I get great leftovers.

the STAR claims I'm having a secret
affair with Michael Jackson's llama.

I like the Chinese ambassador.
Any country that eats dogs
is okay with me.

Sometimes I jam with the President.
He plays saxophone, I play piano.

I lost my wind-up spider.

Yesterday, in the attic, I found an old bowl with "Checkers" written on it. I wonder what it means?

Last night, the President and I slipped away for a few McNuggets. And some nachos and a bowl of yogurt- covered raisins. And a pizza, a bag of sour- cream-and-onion-flavored potato chips, a bag of jalapeño-flavored potato chips, another order of nachos, some Gummi Bears, and a box of glazed donuts. And some more nachos.

I've seen the President nude.

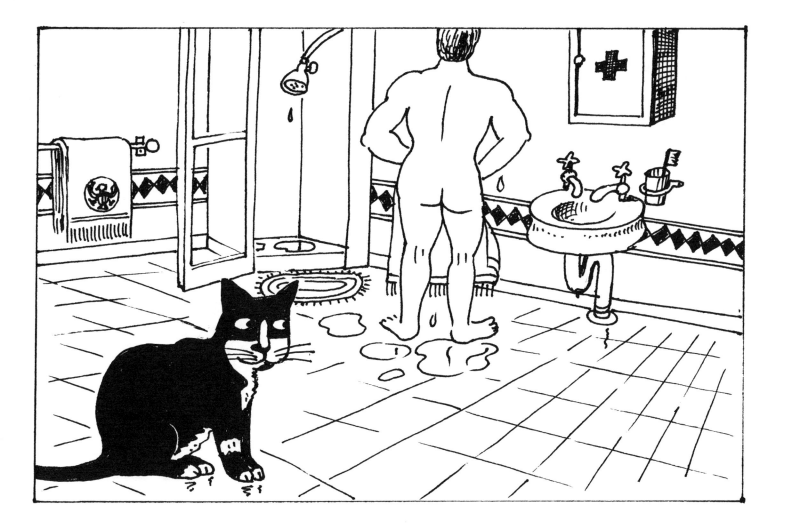

Sometimes the President plays his BLIND FAITH album so loud I have to leave the room.

I worked on the budget this week.

Look what I found! A cheesy book cashing in on White House pets. Some people will do anything for money.

Sam Donaldson stepped on my tail.

"Didn't inhale." Really! I could have come up with a better answer, and I'm a cat.

Every now and then, when you're wondering how to pay off a four-trillion-dollar national debt plus an extra sixty billion Bush claims he "forgot" to mention and you're worried about a sluggish economy and rising unemployment and a crumbling infrastructure and global warming and carjacking and the banks are going under and the schools are getting worse and AIDS is out of control and you're turning back boatloads of Haitians and you still haven't put together a decent health plan and Gore is on your case to save some little spotted owl up in Oregon and you'll probably have to raise taxes on the middle class even though you swore you'd cut them and maybe tax gasoline too which is going to send your approval rating into single digits and every day something weird happens in Bosnia and Somalia and Iraq and the C.I.A. confirmed that Pakistan has seven nuclear bombs and they're not sure but Iran may even have one or two, it's quite soothing to just sit and pet a cat.

Behind every great man, there's a great pet.

I'm bored. Time to break some more china.